OUR DIGITAL PLANET

5/17

Using Digital Technology

by Ben Hubbard

capstone

To contact Capstone Global Library please phone 800-747-4992, or visit our website www.mycapstone.com

Edited by Nikki Potts
Designed by Sarah Bennett
Picture research by Ruth Smith
Production by Laura Manthe
Originated by Capstone Global Library Limited
Printed and bound in China
007875

Library of Congress Cataloging-in-Publication Data
Names: Hubbard, Ben, 1973- author.
Title: Using digital technology / by Ben Hubbard.
Description: North Mankato, Minnesota : Heinemann Raintree, a Capstone imprint, [2017] | Series: Heinemann read and learn. Our digital planet | Audience: Ages 6–8. | Audience: K to grade 3. | Includes bibliographical references and index.
Identifiers: LCCN 2016029364| ISBN 9781484635971 (library binding) | ISBN 9781484636015 (paperback) | ISBN 9781484636138 (ebook (pdf))
Subjects: LCSH: Internet—Juvenile literature. | Computers and children—Juvenile literature.
Classification: LCC TK5105.875.I57 H74 2017 | DDC 004.67/8—dc23
LC record available at https://lccn.loc.gov/2016029364

Acknowledgements
We would like to thank the following for permission to reproduce photographs: Dreamstime: Tomnex, 10; Shutterstock: Bambax, 22 (e-book), Bloomua, 8, GagliardiImages, 19, Georgejmclittle, 13, 22 (streaming), back cover left, Iryna Tiumentseva, 18, Monkey Business Images, 5, Nata-Lia, 4, Nednapa Sopasuntorn, 20, Nikolaeva, cover design element, interior design element, ProStockStudio, cover, Rawpixel.com, 6, 11, 17, 22 (cloud), 22 (download), scyther5, 22 (social media), sirikorn thamniyom, 12, Stefano Garau, 9, back cover right, Twin Design, 22 (application), Tyler Olson, 21 Uber Images, 16, Vinne, 14, waldru, 15; Thinkstock: AndreyPopov, 7

We would like to thank Matt Anniss for his invaluable help in the preparation of this book.

Every effort has been made to contact copyright holders of material reproduced in this book. Any omissions will be rectified in subsequent printings if notice is given to the publisher.

Contents

Some words are shown in bold, **like this**.
You can find them in the glossary on page 22.

How Do We Use Computers?

Computers come in many shapes and sizes. Tablets, laptops, and smart phones are all computers.

We use computers for many different reasons. We play games on computers. We can also use computers to help with schoolwork.

How Do We Connect with Computers?

People connect in many ways using computers. We can write to each other using **social media**.

We can share files using e-mail. We can also make voice and video calls with messaging programs.

What Are Programs and Apps?

A computer runs a program to carry out a set of tasks. Special programs called **applications** let us listen to music, search the Internet, write and save documents, and more.

An "app" is an application for tablets and smart phones. Apps are usually simpler than programs designed for larger computers.

How Do We Use the Internet?

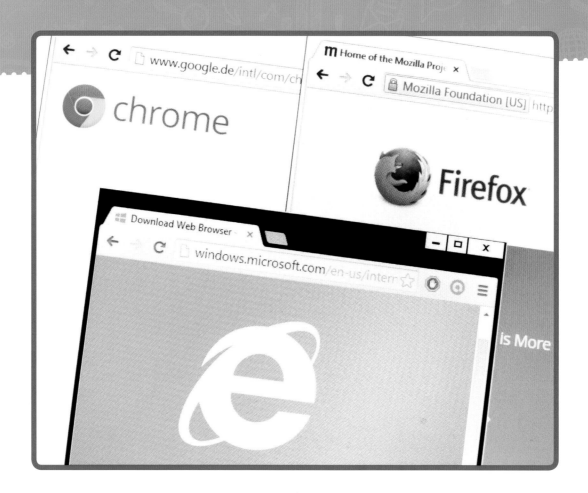

To visit a website, we type its web address into an **application** called a web browser. Some popular browsers are Firefox and Chrome.

We can also search for information by typing words into a search engine. Popular search engines include Google and Bing.

How Do We Get Movies and Music?

Files such as music, movies, and **e-books** can be **downloaded** from the Internet. We can store these files on our computers.

Music, movies, and TV shows can also be "**streamed**" from the Internet. You can watch or listen to streamed files whenever you like, but they cannot be stored.

Where Do We Store Files?

Computers are like digital filing cabinets that store our files. We organize our files by putting them into folders. Files can also be stored in the "**cloud**."

We can then access our cloud files from anywhere, on any computer that is connected to the Internet.

What Are Word and Number Files?

Many people use word processing **applications** to type documents on a computer. These text files can be created for school, home, and work.

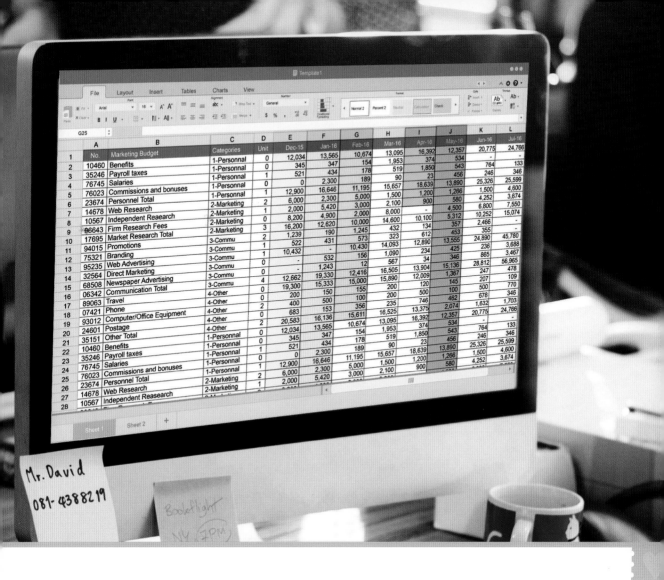

Spreadsheets are another type of file.
They are used to store numbers and
do math.

How Do We Play Games?

There are many different computer games. Some are action and sports games.

Others are puzzles and quizzes.
Games can be played alone or
with other people.

Can We Design Our Own Applications?

Some **applications** let us create our own music, movies, and artwork. There are even applications to design our own apps!

Many people start a career in computers
by designing their own apps.

Glossary

 **application** computer program that performs a certain task

 **cloud** where information is kept on large computers; the information can be accessed from anywhere, anytime

 **download** transferring a copy of a file from the Internet to your computer

 **e-book** electronic book that can be read on a computer

 **social media** form of online communication where users create online communities to share information, ideas, messages, etc.

 **streaming** sending sounds or moving pictures over the Internet, straight to your computer

Find Out More

Books

Gray, Leon. *How Does Cloud Computing Work?* High-Tech Science. New York: Gareth Stevens Publishing, 2014.

La Bella, Laura. *How Do I Use a Database?* Research Tools You Can Use. New York: Britannica Educational Publishing, 2015.

Yearling, Tricia. *Computers: What They Are and How to Use Them.* Zoom in on Technology. New York: Enslow Publishing, 2016.

Internet Sites

Facthound offers a safe, fun way to find Internet sites related to this book. All of the sites on Facthound have been researched by our staff.

Here's all you do:
Visit *www.facthound.com*
Type in this code: 9781484635971

Index